# the **D**EMOCRATIC **S**TATE of **E**NVIRONMENT *INTIMATE MINDS*

RAMZI F. SAAB

ARCHWAY
PUBLISHING

Archway Publishing books may be ordered through booksellers or by contacting:

Archway Publishing
1663 Liberty Drive
Bloomington, IN 47403
www.archwaypublishing.com
1 (888) 242-5904

Because of the dynamic nature of the Internet, any web addresses or links contained in this book may have changed since publication and may no longer be valid. The views expressed in this work are solely those of the author and do not necessarily reflect the views of the publisher, and the publisher hereby disclaims any responsibility for them.

Any people depicted in stock imagery provided by Thinkstock are models, and such images are being used for illustrative purposes only. Certain stock imagery © Thinkstock.

ISBN: 978-1-4808-4116-1 (sc)
ISBN: 978-1-4808-4117-8 (e)

Library of Congress Control Number: 2016920727

Print information available on the last page.

Archway Publishing rev. date: 01/24/2017

# Contents

This book became a reality after the support and hard work of

Nahida Saab
Susan Casmier
Farah Saab
Ghassan H. Saab
Salim Zouheiry
Lena Basmajian
Elie Maalouf
Issam Naaman
Walid Salman

Thank you
Ramzi Saab

# FOREWORD

I met Ramzi Saab when I was teaching at DeVry Institute of Technology (now DeVry University) in Los Angeles, California. Ramzi was a student, although he probably should have been a teacher. He was probably the most inquisitive, talkative, friendly student I ever had. In a fairly short time we became friends. Unfortunately, because of the immigration laws, he had to go back to Lebanon, where he has lived until the present time. I was thrilled to finally get a contact e-mail address for him some years later because there was always some kind of disaster going on in Lebanon, and I worried about him. Turns out he survived and had married and had two beautiful children, whom I have seen thanks to Facebook. Sometime later he told me he had written a book and wanted me to make corrections of his English.

I read this book that he calls science fiction and I called a utopian suggestion to improve the world. He postulated a lot of ideas I disagreed with, and rather than focusing on the whole, I picked at little parts of the book. Then he sent me a story called *Intimate Minds*, a predictable story about two extraordinary people. I thought it was kind of corny. I didn't take it seriously. Meanwhile, I plugged away at making corrections and suggestions, such as, "I would omit this entire paragraph." Always polite and respectful, Ramzi ignored my suggestions and to some extent my corrections. I ended up correcting the grammar, spelling, sentence structure, etc., three times. In the process, I came to respect his suggestion about the possible solutions presented in the *Democratic State of Environment*.

*The Democratic State of Environment and the Intimate Minds* is a most *thought-provoking* book. Especially now, its suggestions are needed, and oh, how I wish they could be realized. As I write this, we have just witnessed another mass shooting about fifty miles from where I sit.

Another crazy man and woman killed fourteen people and wounded many more in San Bernardino, California. Last month, it was Paris, Nigeria, and Lebanon. Right now, the heads of states of the world are meeting to put an end to climate warming, while the US Congress (bought and paid for by the American oil industry) refuses to back up the president, who wants to sign a pact to save the world. We literally have murder and mayhem every day in our world. Ramzi Saab has a workable, feasible idea to save it. This book deserves a close look. Our world needs a global "soft revolution," as Mr. Saab calls it, to change its ways before our planet is unlivable and before everyone is dead or too terrorized to enjoy life.

Susan Casmier
Los Angeles, California

# INTRODUCTION

## The Democratic State of Environment
## Intimate Minds

Every day we read about many horrible events of humans harming other humans, or animals, or the land. American police shoot innocent people; bands of Islamic terrorists kidnap girls to punish them for going to school. Large corporations poison the land so they can get more yields out of the earth without thought for what the future may hold for the land or the humans who consume those crops or the animals that might graze on that land. We dig for oil and gas and corrupt the water nearby. On it goes: the rich get richer; the poor get desperately poorer. Teachers aren't respected. Human life isn't respected. Some Christian pastors hate gays. People disrespect the US president because he is black. People don't believe in science when scientific fact conflicts with stories in the Bible. Some Israelis don't think that Israeli Muslims or Palestinian Christians should have equal rights in that country. These negative attitudes and events intensify every day. So it is time for a plan for living together peacefully on this earth with respect for each other, for the land, and for clean water.

I developed a plan that proposes some solutions I will present in this booklet in the form of a group of serious suggestions and a fictional story. I wanted to find answers or solutions for most of humanity's problems in the areas of politics, economy, housing, justice, ethics, and happiness. I haven't included any scientific research or outstanding discoveries. The ideas and answers resulted from my life that I have lived on three continents and where I experienced the best of the best and the worst of the worst in life. I was happy most of the time because I managed to turn my pains into challenges and struggles into victories, acceptance, and meditation … And now, after fifty years, I ask myself why.

This book can be best classified as political and social science fiction in which I put forth my suggestions for improving the state of humanity. If I had the chance to live my life over again, I would like to be a citizen in a Democratic State of Environment.

Religion and philosophy are attempts to understand the ups and downs of human existence. Religion is based on an illogical premise and uses illogical derivations to reach toward good aims. Philosophy is also based on an illogical premise, but it uses logical derivations to reach its good aims. Our starting point will be the beauty, perfection, and continuity of nature, for this is a truth that does not need any proof.

Throughout history, all the political, religious, and philosophical movements needed and will always need money, wars, and weapons to achieve their goals. Those same things will be needed to prevent these movements. If we continue human life as it is, pain and the destruction of nature will continue. To reject war, terrorism, and the destruction of the environment for human comfort would require a soft revolution, exactly what is required to save our environment and ourselves. The soft revolution is a new concept where revolutions have no enemy and need no leader and do not require killing or destruction.

# First Transformation

## Definition

A soft revolution is the only means for achieving the Democratic State of Environment *without* bloodshed and through the first global referendum. The soft revolution is accomplished in three consecutive steps. The first is constructing an implementing military force.* The second step is nationalizing the military and law schools. The third is converting political parties into universities.

Before explaining and expanding upon the idea of the soft revolution, it is necessary to give new definitions to the concepts of a "state" and "homeland." It is necessary to get rid of all the inherited prejudice of the last four thousand years of shining wars and shameful glories.

## Our New Definition of State

By *state* I mean a law of human cooperation whose purpose is to secure the source and path of fresh water and the just use of the land, water, raw materials, and energy in the area of the water path.*

The *homeland* is a piece of land on which the state is built. This piece of land may expand or shrink depending on the strength of the state. Here we will change the concept and name of the *homeland;* it will be referred to as *the water path.*

1

## Definition of Water Path

The water path is a fair natural division of the globe, which allows the formation of relatively equal states.

These new definitions confirm the fact that we are talking about a comprehensive radical movement, where we will free the land from the "right" to fight over it, and we will free the state from being civil, religious, national, ethnic, or ideological. And we will force justice among states as a prerequisite to justice among individuals.

Next, we will explain and define the three steps of the soft revolution, but we have to keep in mind that the new concepts might appear vague or complicated in the beginning and will clear up as you go along.

## First Step—Constructing an Implementing Military Force

In the third world, we have become familiar with the idea of military coup d'états. And now we are living in the era of launching wars for the sake of changing regimes, while in the rest of the world, huge fortunes control the lives of people and sedate them to an extent that makes them unaware of the growing dangers around them. For example, September 11 was a result of miscalculated policy in Afghanistan. (If the first plane succeeded in hitting the pentagon and then the other planes hit the towers, we can consider it a pure terrorist attack, but this was not the case.)

Based on the above, there came a need to build a coalition of huge, effective armies to build an invincible military force financed by wealthy countries such as the United States, Russia, China, the UK, France, and Germany, whose mission is to enforce new changes in the world order.

According to these new changes, wars between states would be considered illegal; *demographic wars would be considered crimes against humanity.* Freedom and justice would be governed by the safety of the environment.

The environment should be considered the source of all legislation in our new state.

All the struggles that have already taken place in the world, like the Second World War, will turn out to be ineffective because they caused more damage and pain than progress and achievements. Getting rid of Hitler's regime was a necessity, of course, but it could have been achieved in a smaller, more intelligent manner. As for the struggles that are still going on, like the Jewish-Arab struggle, these are kept going because a third party benefits. *This is not data; it is more likely the author's feeling, which is so close to certainty.* Wars were responsible for most of my personal problems. I will feel much better if I accuse the third party of promoting wars.

Now that we have the ability to use modern technology to simulate wars and to predict their military, economic, environmental, and psychological outcomes, we must construct an *implementing military force,* which will start its mission only after explaining the new regime and getting its authorization from *the first international referendum.* This means that the military will take over, but only after gaining permission through the first international referendum.

This military force, which has all the possible powers that one can imagine, will ensure a peaceful transformation to the new system *and back* to the old system if the new did not work well. A deep look to the way current governments work gives us a clear realization of the extent that the military has influence over the system. All that we are changing is that it will be elected.

## Second Step—Nationalization of Military and Law Schools

Nationalization, to those who don't know, is to take the ownership away from individuals or private companies and give it to the new state.[1] Here we are going to modify the name of the law school where it will be:

A. The School of Law and State Management. In this college, law will be taught as it has already been. Also what is new in law school is the teaching of state management, which includes the following:

- Energy
- Raw material
- Public health
- Social services
- Transportation
- Finance
- Foreign affairs
- Tourism
- Education, culture, and reservations
- Economy

    These areas of study become the cabinet that governs the state. Each area has a cabinet member.

- Internal affairs (includes housing, police, immigration, customs) become the responsibility of the vice president.
- Environment and media become the responsibility of the president.

---

[1] When we refer to the new state, we mean one of the fifteen new states, which are suggested in the third transformation.

The mission of this college, in addition to teaching, is to graduate lawyers who will then have the right to run for positions in judicial authority and executive authority, both central and local. Gaining admittance to this college will be accomplished by winning a local election. In the current systems, you can enter law school if you choose to. In the D.S.E., you have to be elected by the community you live with and that knows you very well. Local elections will assign the graduated lawyers to positions of the executive local authority, and the general elections will assign lawyers to the executive central government. Each lawyer who gets elected into an executive position will lose the right to vote or to run for positions in the judicial authority. The half yearly referendum will renew or impeach any elected personnel. The rest of the lawyers will turn into an elected committee, which will elect members from within to fill the positions of the judicial local and central authority. In this college, specialization is allowed only in higher education levels. Achieving a high education level (like a master's degree or PhD) is a prerequisite to run for the higher positions in the executive and judicial authorities.

B. Military School—In this school, military science and training would be taught as they are presently. Military sciences will include the following subjects:

- Scientific research
- Natural disasters
- Crisis management
- Jails and rehabilitation centers
- Defending positions
- Assisting judges
- Information and communication
- Military judicial
- Military training

One can gain admission to this college only through local election. The graduate will lose the right to share in the public local and central elections. Promotions of military personnel will be decided by internal voting of the military. Running for higher positions would require a higher level of education.

## Third Step—Converting Political Parties into Universities

The government is the only body that has the right to run *law* and *military* universities. Any other universities or major subjects are restricted to the private sector. For example, the government cannot have a university to teach medicine, engineering, philosophy, history, or any majors other than law and military.

In this way, any person who has a religious, philosophical, or political belief can start a university instead of a political party (for example, the Christian University, the Hebrew University, Communist University, etc.).

These private universities will have the same mission they already had. Their important additional mission would be to take the job of the senators in preparing and promoting legislation and sending it to the half-yearly referendum to implement it as a new law.

In this transformation, we can protect the future of the youth, who often have the tendency to want to change everything right away while sometimes ending up ruining their own lives in stupid or miscalculated revolution. In this new system a person/student can have his or her revolution within the university and get university credit for it.

*Parliaments will be unnecessary.* We can keep an eye on the executive branch through the elected judicial authority, and the legislation will be prepared at the universities. Then the half-yearly referendum will be responsible for implementing the legislation.

The most beautiful part of this suggestion is to get rid of the parliaments and congresses that have caused much of the corruption and injustice in this world.

Note: without bloodshed, wouldn't you consider that to be soft?

# Intimate Minds

**the first episode**

In Afghanistan, in the year 2023, a baby boy called Mohammad is born.

The country lies under the occupation of the United States, a country that is much larger and far away, with a different religion, lifestyle, and social values. His mother was sick and died because she lacked medical care. His father worked for the town's chief, and he did not have the time to take care of his child, so the boy was raised by his uncle. Mohammad was a very bright boy and was able to solve a lot of his life's problems alone using his creative imagination and a strange intuition.

In the United States, in the same year, a baby girl called Sally was born. Her mother was not able to get pregnant naturally, so she used in-vitro fertilization. Unfortunately, she died during Sally's birth. All the technology of the well-developed country could not save her life.

Sally's father was the owner of the largest computer company in the world. After his wife's death, he was devoted to raising Sally. Sally was very bright and was able to solve her problems using her creativity and a strange intuition.

*To be continued on page 18…*

# SECOND TRANSFORMATION

## The Global Nature of the Democratic State Of Environment (D.S.E.)

The world has known many attempts to change the political and economic regimes, and they all occurred under military, economic, religious, and/or demographic struggles.

*Demographic wars were the most dangerous of all.* Demographic wars are launched by a group of people against another group by increasing the birth rate and using the increased population to dominate the minorities.

Under these struggles, humanity failed to discern which of the theories were right and wrong. Had they agreed on the contradiction between humanity and the idea of survival of the fittest (since this idea cannot stand in the presence of the variety of intelligence, physical abilities, and endurance of humans), they would have seen that survival would be the result of harmonizing human abilities, not through human struggles.

Therefore, we have to create a global understanding that allows different theories to prove themselves without destroying the universe in the process.

Through "soft revolution" we can come to agree on this global understanding, based on these five elements:

1. The implementing force
2. The relatively equal states
3. Globalization of law of individual ownership rights

4.  Globalization of election law
5.  Globalization of organic farming

## THE IMPLEMENTING FORCE

We showed in the previous chapters the methods of forming this force, and here we will talk about the importance of its continuity and how to improve its quality.

This force is formed by a balanced participation from all the new D.S.E. states. It may start as a traditional military force, but it will transform with time to be a new phenomenon in the history of humankind because it will be a result of the first elected military force that enjoys a complete financial and judicial independence, and it does not submit to the political and judicial authorities except by obeying the orders within its predescribed authorities.

To those who are worried that the military will never give up power, I have to remind them here that this elected military is under the impeachment power of the people.

## THE RELATIVELY EQUAL STATE

As it was defined, the new homeland, the fair division of the globe, allows the formation of relatively equal states in size and in power to prevent the greed that has always been a reason for international wars. This relatively equal state can be a reason that self-sufficient states would reduce the need for international trade, which is also a reason for wars.

Greed among states in international trade is one of the most important causes of corruption and injustice.

## Globalized Law of Individual Ownership Rights

Laws of ownership differ among countries of different political systems in the world. The right of the individual's ownership varies, so in some states an individual can have the right to own the metals and oil underneath his property, while in some other states an individual cannot even have the right to own the surface of a lot.

As for the law that we are suggesting, ownership rights should be composed of the following major ideas:

- Each individual would have the right to own a lot suitable to build a house. This ownership would be permanent.
- The size of the lot should be enough to allow house farming.[2]
- The individual would not have the right to own what is underneath the property (metals or oil) or the seashore or river banks or any other natural water surface.
- The individual's wealth should not exceed what would be set by the international ethics conference, $200 million, for example.
- Personal wealth should not be less than the ability to get proper nutrition and basic education and health care.

It will be up to the universities to study such laws and propose them through the global referendum.

## Globalized Election Law

There is no doubt that democracy is the best form of government that politics and civil rights movements have created since the beginning of history. However, evil forces have historically used democracy for their goals and evil aims through a devil oligarchy disguised as election law.

---

[2] House farming is the farming activity around the house for a variety of produce for personal consumption, not for trade.

Many secret recipes are used in different parts of the world to design election laws that make the results of the election predetermined.

My explanation of the rules of election law is found in the Ninth and Tenth Transformation; however, I want to explain here the need for globalizing election laws. Globalization ensures the protection of the election law from the struggle over authority, and from the variation in the public mood that is strongly influenced by privately financed media. Furthermore, globalization guarantees the balance in international relations and protects minorities from the effect of the strong religious and ideological majorities.

## Globalized Organic Farming

The subject of organic farming will be addressed in the Eighth Transformation. However, the need for globalizing organic farming lies in ensuring balance in the global economy, since the difference in the power of production between organic farming and its competitor is way too large. In addition, the migratory routes of birds and butterflies as well the wind streams, all of which cross national boundaries, influence the quality of produce and create another reason for globalization.

# THIRD TRANSFORMATION

## Harmonizing Political and Natural World Map

NUMBERS    SUGGESTED STATES
X's        GLOBAL NATURAL RESERVATIONS

These divisions are not final, nor the number of states. It will be the job of the experts to divide the planet according to the water resources.

The people of each state will give their state its name. Keep in mind that this book is not suggesting a global government. It is trying to direct the attention to some aspects that *must* be globalized to ensure the safety of the planet and to some other aspects that *must not* be globalized to ensure the freedom, diversity, and happiness of the people.

# Fourth Transformation

## The Reservations System

This system represents the method that allows the old countries to integrate into the new fifteen countries. Harmonization between this system and the new cities (Fifth Transformation) will eliminate the need for having different kinds of regimes and states that have caused all the struggles and misery that pressured the human spirit and pushed it away from its humanity.

The integration between ethnicity and religion has caused the largest problems, so we needed to negotiate with God and his prophets to design an election law or to build a highway. Here we are calling the followers of the ethnic religions or the religions of ethnic groups to decide the methods by which they will join the new state. Therefore, they have to choose between the ethnicity or the religion to protect their culture. There will be five kinds of new cities in which they should find what satisfies their ambitions. (This is explained in the Fifth Transformation.)

The reservation system is made up of four types: ethnic or national, religious, historical, and natural. Each of these reservations should establish its own methods to finance itself.

## Ethnic or National Reservation

At various times in history, humans have witnessed the creation of variety of ethnic and national groups. Some of them were superior and some were not and some were exactly the opposite, but there was always a reason for struggles and wars because of the feeling of superiority that controlled its relations with any other groups, as well as the feeling of unquestioned ownership of land and the desire to control more land and more people.

Ethnic groups are formed by direct blood relation between a group of people. Its circumstances allowed it to avoid mixing with others. Nationalities were a result of mixing different ethnic groups on particular pieces of land. This mixing was mostly exploitation and spiritual and physical pains, and slavery. When exploitation stops with one group, it starts with another.

We cannot imagine that what was built by history could be destroyed easily, because some of these nationalities and ethnic groups had built a relationship among its members, and in some cases between the members and the land. It may take thousands of years to undo these relationships, possibly never.

But in our Democratic State of Environment, it is possible for these nationalities or ethnic groups to merge completely into the new state by individual choice or to get into the reservation system. To see how it works, see the following explanation:

It is possible through traditional and historical rights to consider some pieces of lands as ethnic or national reservations (Jerusalem, for example), so these groups can reserve their memories and distinguishing character. These reservations can be used for housing the individual, if this housing doesn't violate the laws of protecting the environment from pollution and from demographic warfare.

This reservation can be built by a referendum, after which the individuals may choose to keep their old nationality or ethnicity.

Financing will be done independently from the general revenue. The financial responsibility falls on the individuals who choose to keep the nationality or the ethnicity. Negotiation will be done with the new state to control the level of production inside the reservation, which profits should not exceed the cost of the reservation except to acceptable levels.

## RELIGIOUS RESERVATION

The idea of having a religious reservation is to solve one of the greatest and most complicated problems of humanity. Different kinds of religions played a major role in raising the level of human lives until religion started to interfere in the formation of old states.

Because of that interference, great struggles appear between the civil authorities and the religious authorities. For example, the church does not need any law to prohibit abortion, since every member of the church knows that abortion is not good. The state does not need a law that allows abortion. All it needs is to be sure that the decision to abort was made willingly by the pregnant woman herself, unless she and her male partner had an agreement to raise a child together, in which case he should provide a document proving that the woman had agreed to motherhood.

With the formation of religious reservations, religious groups can ensure the freedom of movement and of the issues that concern them. The religious reservations can be used for housing if it was under the authority of the new state and falls under the same rules as the national and ethnic reservations, also in taxation and productivity. But if it was an international religious reservation, it cannot be used for housing except for the clergy or the *mashayekh* or the *khalifa* or the *pope* or any other title that will be decided by the religious leaders, as revenue from religious tourism should be distributed among the needy followers of that religion and the followers should finance it without using taxes. Religious reservations should not be allowed to build great fortunes.

Religious reservations can be established following referendums. The international followers of that religion must contribute to the establishment and maintenance of their religious state (for example, Mecca) after an international referendum.

It is not acceptable anymore, after thousands of years of civilization, for faiths to have states built on religious bases that do not benefit the religion in any way but then play a major role in destroying the world.

## Historical Reservations

These reservations will be for limited areas, like the pyramids in Egypt or the Great Wall of China or new things like the Statue of Liberty or places like Buckingham Palace or the palace of the Japanese empire if the individuals who choose to keep their old nationalities decided to keep these palaces as national reservations.

These reservations cannot be used for housing and financing. It will be the mission of the new state, and its revenues go back to the new state.

Forming these reservations can be done based on general referendum, after getting a clearance from referendum the individuals who choose to keep their old nationality or ethnicity.

## Natural Reservations

Natural reservations protect the state of nature, as in national parks, for example.

These reservations can be developed based on general referendum. They cannot be used for housing, or for military bases, although the military can patrol the reservations. All financing for these reservations and its revenues go back to the new state.

# Intimate Minds

**the second episode**

*… Continued from page 8*

The year is 2031. Both babies are eight years old. Sally wanted to swim in the Pacific Ocean, but her dad told her that the ocean had become a drainage for the large city's sewage. He asked the captain of his private yacht to find a location away from the sewage so she could swim in clean water.

Sally asked her dad, "What percentage of clean water is used to carry the dirty water to the ocean?"

Impressed by her question, her dad said, "Well, it's a big percentage, but why are you asking?"

"Why do we have to add clean water to an already wet waste material? Why don't we dry the waste instead, so that it won't be harmful to nature?"

The thought came to Sally's mind through that strange intuition that gave her a feeling that she had contact with another brain. Sally, who had always been a sad baby, for the first time felt proud and pleased with herself.

Mohammad felt embarrassed every time he sat down for dinner at his uncle's home. His uncle's wife always discriminated between him and her own children. One day he asked his father to be present when dinner was served, but his father said, "I can't do that." His father worked at the kitchen of the town's chief.

Mohammad said, "Why don't you let me work with you at the chief's house so we can have meals together?"

Mohammad did work with his father. It was that strange intuition that made him do that. Although the job was boring, it gave him some hope. Mohammad saved some money and went to the big city, where he lost all his savings and could not find his way back to his father. In the big city he met an American soldier, who helped him with food and shelter.

*To be continued on page 31…*

## The New Cities

The development of human civilization throughout history correlated with the need to build great cities until these cities began to house millions. One of the most important reasons for that need was to ensure the safety of great individuals' wealth. And no matter how great the advantages of great cities, the disadvantages are still greater because of the harm great cities can do to the natural environment and to human ethics.

The true value of civilization lies in its ability to continue raising the level of human life; however, any civilization that does not respect the laws of nature and piles up people in high-rise and attached buildings or houses them in the path of rivers or near beaches to face tsunamis is not raising the level of human life, but lowering it.

Ignorance of the law is not an excuse.

Ignorance of law of nature means what?

Therefore, one of the most important duties of the Democratic State of Environment is to break up these cities and redistribute their population in a way that will not harm the environment or the civilization but will respect the laws of nature by making smaller cities.

This system of new cities will represent the best solution to build a new civilization that will be capable of continuously raising the level of life.

In our new system, there will be five kinds of new cities. Every individual will have the right to choose the one that matches his or her personality after reaching adulthood.

## CIVIL CITIES

These cities can be established through a decision voted on by the new state and will be organized according to the historically accepted human values that have a global nature—for example, shaking hands, one man marries one woman, the tendency for better education, the desire for wealth and recreation, and the freedom to think.

I will not explain more, since this is a complicated issue and those experts who know how to design civil cities should do their part. And please, dear reader, here we are imagining. In the civil city we can build a church or mosque or a temple if these places will not disturb it in any way. For example, they cannot interfere with traffic or delay it on any religious or ethnic or national occasion.

In the civil cities, anybody can promote any religion or philosophy or political issues as far as it does not violate the laws of protecting children and decency.

## ETHNIC OR NATIONAL CITIES

These cities can be established by a decision of the new state and will be based on the culture of the ethnic group or the nationality for designing the internal laws and ethics. These cities will guarantee the freedom of choice in the new state, and even if the choice is racist, it will not create a threat to humanity or to the natural environment. (The KKK can have its own city.)

It will be up to the local government of the city to allow or prohibit religious and philosophical and political beliefs.

## Religious Cities

These cities can be established by a decision of the new state based on what the particular religion determines, for example, a Catholic city, an Orthodox Jewish city, or Shiaa Muslim city. These kinds of cities will guarantee the freedom of religious activities of all kinds, including laws of marriage and heritage and what follows.

In these cities one could hear Muslims praying over loudspeakers, and the Christians can ring their loud bells all over town.

It will be up to the local government in these cities to allow or prohibit the promotion of other religions or philosophies or political views, and it will be decided by the local government if there should be a particular dress code or separation between males and females or any other issues that concern the religion followers.

## Ideological Cities

These cities can be built by a decision of the new state based on individuals' requests, which should reach the number predecided by the international ethics conference. (This is explained in the Ninth Transformation.)

In this kind of city, people who have different ways of living, which includes what could be unacceptable by others, or people who don't believe in education or production or any other issue, can live their lives. For example, we can have a communist city or a Nazi city or a city for gays or a city for those who don't believe in a state or even a city for those who consider dolphins as citizens.

It is up to the local government of these cities to accept or prohibit religious or philosophical or political promotions.

## Migrants' Cities

These cities can be established by a decision of the new state if it concerns members of a nomadic migrating tribe or group who depends on travel as a way of life. They may already have their historical reservations. But if individuals made a number of requests that match the predefined number by the international ethics conference, a new migrant city will be established covering an area in which they are free to travel and present no danger to others or to the environment.

## A Brainstorm in the New Cities

**Storm:** In our new state, the age of adulthood means joining the university and recognizing or refusing the statehood. Recognizing means swearing, in the presence of a judge, in a special ceremony for every individual, where the individual will state that he or she has studied and accepted the general law. Then the citizen will choose the kind of city that matches the spirit. This means the person is simply not a citizen until he or she swears to have studied and accepted the general law.

**Storm**: In our new state, no local authority can prohibit citizens from living in any kind of city, even if they do not believe in the same religion or are not from the same nationality, as long as they accept the local laws.

**Storm:** The new city is formed from a group of final residential lots that cannot be used to build or enlarge roads, and their ownership is final and cannot be sold. These lots must be large enough to allow house farming, and they must be in areas safe from floods, tsunamis, or forest fires. They are protected from taxation. They can be exchanged if the neighbors agree and can be inherited without any taxation.

**Storm**: Every new city has the right to refuse any law issued by the new state if the law is not of an environmental nature, and in return the city cannot benefit from the refused law.

**Storm:** The population of the new cities should not exceed one hundred thousand, and when that number is approached, building a new city is suggested if there is no evidence of demographic warfare.

**Storm**: All new cities should obey the laws issued by the new state if these laws have an environmental or military nature. So, for example, no city is allowed to build an old sewer system. Instead, it will have the new immediate-drying system, which uses a nearby forest designated for that next to any city or industrial, military, or tourist complex. Here we leave to the experts the evaluation of the idea and discover the benefits of using less water, better hygiene, fewer detergents, and fewer pesticides.

Are you ready to enter the new house?

# Sixth Transformation

## Global Natural Reservations and International Committees

It is necessary to maintain some parts of the globe as natural reservations where no residences should be built. Nor should these reserved lands be used as a source for oil or other raw material.

The international implementing military force patrols these areas to protect them from settlements. This military force may not build any kind of base in these territories.

It is possible to have some international religious reservations, for example the Vatican, Mecca, or Jerusalem. Further, these reservations can enjoy the protection of the international military force without allowing the force to enter the reservations or to interfere with its policies.

The North Pole and the South Pole and the open oceans, including the little islands and some parts of the Himalayan Mountains, Tibet, parts of the African deserts, and parts of Siberia, should be considered as global natural reservations, primarily to encourage humankind to feel that they are not the unquestioned owners of this planet.

And in harmony with our tendency to create smaller governments, the international committees should also be small, so in addition to the international implementing force, we will need only the global ethics conference.

This conference will be invited only when needed by any one of the fifteen presidents. It will not have any budget. It will be formed by the fifteen leaders of the judicial system, who will have the deciding authority of the conference through open voting. Such voting will be allowed by the consulting authority of the conference, which will include the presidents of all universities in the world.

The main mission of this committee is to allow or prohibit scientific research, so it will not present a threat to the safety of the globe or the future of humanity. In addition, it will prohibit conflicts and determine the maximum limit of a personal fortune.

**Good-Bye United Nations.**

Here I will leave it to the reader to think about the volume of the UN's achievements compared with the amount of money spent and the level of democracy practiced by the UN Security Council.

It was mentioned in the beginning of this book that the implementing military force is one of the requirements of the soft revolution, and here we will add to that explanation that this force will be formed in a balanced way by all of the fifteen new states. Here we should remind ourselves that the military in these new states is elected and has independent taxing systems, so there will be no need to finance the international force.

As the military force in the new states obey the decisions of the ethics conference, so the international military force will obey the decisions of the global ethics conference as long as they do not contradict the reason for which the force was formed. It was formed by the first global referendum and cannot be changed or revoked except through the same global referendum.

# Seventh Transformation

### The Real Fortune

The real fortune is the most dangerous truth approached in this book. It all started when men used food, dress, and jewelry to show off at the beginning of history. These items of value became currency (hard and easy), real estate, stock market shares, and an endless chain of money mazes.

Most wealth is an illusion that appears very similar to the truth because of its long standing. Many incidents exposed this illusion; still nobody gave it the attention it deserves. From the recession and the depression to the banks' failures, the smart people's reaction was always to buy gold and properties.

Today, with all the technology we have, it is not a secret that if someone decides to dig out gold in huge quantities, it will lose its value. Likewise, flooding the market with diamonds would reduce their value tremendously. If someone had the complete genetic map of the human body, nobody would have the right to question his or her capabilities.

I believe the following: the real fortune is only in these three elements:

1. Land to farm
2. A source of fresh water
3. A source of renewable energy

Everything else is an illusion.

And these fortunes should be subject to fair spreading and reservation through the Democratic State of Environment.

# Eighth Transformation

It has been about forty years since I began trying to understand economic systems. But I continued to fail. For that reason I decided to design my own private system. To do that, and to stay in harmony with the current systems, I decided to design my system by shopping. Since I am a failure in amassing a fortune, and since I am not an expert in economics, the best way I can describe myself is that I am an economic victim.

We will start with the environment, since in our new state, the environment is the source of all legislation. Economy is composed of the following elements: agriculture, agriculture manufacturing, manufacturing, trading, finance, media, and others. Each one of these elements has its negative effect on the environment. Let's start with criminal farming (nonorganic farming). It requires a lot of energy and machinery, chemical nutrients, and pesticides, but all these are harmful to the environment. Criminal farming has allowed production of huge amounts of food that created demographic wars. We have to remind ourselves that demographic wars are more dangerous to humanity than nuclear wars or germ warfare or any other kind of warfare. In agriculture manufacturing there is a lot of consumption of the earth's energy and packing material. Here I have to say something so I can feel better: there is a big difference between old products and new ones. I question moving from the old to the new since the old products were much better and had art and a human touch to them. We will not talk about the consumption of raw material because we don't want to challenge the huge corporations.

Then you have the money, advertisement, insurance, and world trade. Most of these trades are based on offer and demand, which encourages and creates corruption and injustice.

Now let's talk about shopping.

In my new system, the state does not have the right to perform any kind of productivity since production is an exclusive right of the private sector, and the state's role is limited to supervision, coordination, and delegation of missions.

I have to apologize to the communists and the socialists.

In our new state, production is divided into two parts, where production of energy and essential raw materials will be made by the private sector through a contract with the government, which will decide the amount of production and the selling price. That is to ensure the safety of the environment and fairness in providing job opportunities to all people and most importantly to guarantee the rights of unborn generations.

I apologize to the capitalists.

As for the second division, which includes all other products, it will be up to the private sector and the market movement to control the amounts produced and the selling prices.

I apologize to the communists and anybody else who would like to see me apologize.

In our new system, local trade will grow, and international trade will depend on need because it imposes a heavy load on the environment and the consumer. In our new system, we don't need to have many kinds of corporations since there is only one way to pay taxes (military, judicial, and general): a percentage of what went into one's bank account over the last three months. This bank account might be personal for any employee, a salary, or an account of an owner or owners of a company (i.e., profits). We cannot exchange money in our new system except through banks.

The environment does not love cash, nor does ethics. Without the cost of making coins, we will have more money to solve many problems, and without the operation costs of the IRS, we can replant the African desert. Now we can talk about demand prior to production.

Through modern technology we can now show the shape, color, and all specifications and methods of operation of any product before even manufacturing it. There will be no losing companies. However, if a business enterprise fails to profit, it will close.

No bankruptcy.

No offer and demand.

Offer, sell, produce, and get profit.

I love the environment!

In order to give the book a happy ending, we have to talk about money.

## DEFINITION

Money is a contract of fixed value between a citizen and a bank. It is used to replace services and things. Its fixed value is decided by the government through comparing it with an amount of energy. If I have five dollars in my pocket, I don't have any idea what value it will be at in five days. Instead, I will have a bill whose value is 5KWatt of energy and maybe we can call it "Power Me."

I love money!

# Intimate Minds

**the third episode**

*… Continued from page 18*

The year was 2035. Both kids were twelve years old. Sally was a strange student. She liked to attend geography and math classes. She was so excited to study those two subjects as opposed to languages and history, which she disliked. Her father kept visiting her school to try to understand the reason.

Once her father asked her, "Why don't you like history?"

She replied, "Because I'm not sure if what's written in the history books is true."

Her father said, "I've studied history and used to enjoy the class. It's like listening to an exciting story."

Sally said, "Most of history talks about wars and is written by the living. I cannot meet the dead and ask them about their feelings and their opinions regarding what really happened."

She felt great. It was the same great feeling she got whenever she studied geography and math. She liked clarity. When she thought of leaving school, she heard an inner voice urging her not to. It was that strange intuition once more. "It's not the right time yet. You have to study and learn more."

Mohammad used to visit the soldier who had helped him. During one of the visits, the soldier asked Mohammad to help him put on his clothes because he felt a bit of pain due to a mission he had accomplished. During the process of getting him dressed, the soldier asked Mohammad to hit him on the back, but Mohammad was hesitant.

Then the soldier said, "Please hit me so I feel relieved."

Mohammad replied, "I will, but it's not my fault if you get hurt."

The soldier used to get a kind of sexual satisfaction from the beatings. Mohammad did not get suspicious but rather was confused because the soldier asked him to keep the beatings a secret. The sweets and Western food that the soldier gave Mohammad had a great effect on him. Every time Mohammad thought of getting back home, he heard an inner voice telling him not to. It was that strange intuition again. "It's not time to go back yet."

*To be continued on page 39...*

# Ninth Transformation

## The Real Separation of Authorities

In our new state, all government employees are elected no matter what level or type of job they do, and in whichever of the three branches of government: the executive, the judicial, or the military. Each employee is subject to renewing his or her job or losing it through a half-yearly referendum.

## Executive Authority*

The central presidential committee represents the executive authority, which is elected based on the majors of the university of state management—as mentioned in the soft revolution and in the University of Law and State Management, its job is to implement the laws that are enforced by the general referendum.

The local presidential committee, elected by the local residents, closely implements the laws and enjoys a sort of independence, with the exception of the globalized laws and the laws of the central government that come under the category "environmental" or "military."

## Judicial Authority*

Elected by the public through direct local voting, the judicial authority elects its personnel and leaders. Its specified task is arbitration among citizens and among themselves and the executive and military authorities, as well as punishing the violators, whether they are citizens or members of the executive authority (even should it be the president).

## Military Authority*

Selected by the public through direct local voting, the military authority elects its personnel and leaders. Its mission is to protect the new system and help the civil judges in case they need armed forces and to represent the state in the international implementing military forces. The military authority has the duty to monitor the usage of dangerous materials, and it has the exclusive right for scientific research of subjects, which can be categorized as "unusual," for example: genetics, mining, communication systems, explosive materials, etc. That exclusive right will be given to the military by the state ethics conference, which has the right to allow or prohibit the civil use of the research.

Moreover, the military authority will have its own special judicial system, whose mission is to monitor the job of the military, and if there is a dispute between its members, prosecute its own members only (a military court cannot prosecute a civilian).

## State Ethics Conference*

The state ethics conference's authority will exist only when it is needed. The request to have this conference is the right of the state president or any one of the presidents of universities. This conference has no budget, and its mission is to categorize scientific research between ordinary or unusual subjects, as mentioned in the missions of the military authority.

This authority is composed of the presidents of universities as consultants and the supreme judges as decision makers.

*None of these authorities has the right to execute people.

# Tenth Transformation

## Humans and Authorities

Dear readers,

You may be a believer in democracy as it is practiced, or you may be a supporter of other systems. However, since I don't know, I will explain: the northwestern countries enjoy democracies because the citizens of these countries are pushed by their governments to a continuous comparison of their lives with the lives of the citizens of the unfortunate countries, so they feel secure and don't pay enough attention to the economic troubles, unemployment, and unnecessary wars. They don't know that their governments have established dictatorships in the rest of the world. Here, we are talking about the third world, and since I am a citizen of the third world, I will not explain a lot since I feel the danger from writing such a book would make me kiss my kids good-bye before I publish it.

This world, which is full of loss and misery, is controlled—on a needed basis for a limited time when law and order or economics dictate—by military force, money, secret organizations, and the current democracies. We need somebody to admit failure and say, "Let's do something about it."

We came to realize that military force is the real ruler of the world at the moment (and based on the explanation of "the soft revolution"). We are invited to put this military force under control by turning the moment into a permanent situation but in our state the military force will be an elected one.

In our new system, ethics can nourish and expand and penetrate the newly elected military force, so if we go back to the days of worrying about military power, we will see there is a difference, which is that the new military will *not* have the power to kill!

In our new system, democracy is the responsibility of each citizen. For comparison:

- Democracy in the old system needed two hours of thinking and thirty minutes of work every year from each citizen, on average.
- In our new system, democracy will require twenty hours of thinking and two hours of work every year, plus or minus 5 percent on average.

Don't you think, dear reader, that democracy, which is the best form of government humanity has known, deserves the same time and attention that humans give to their hairstyles?

Now it is time to fix our hair!

✓ First we have to comb our hair, and that will be by categorizing voters into males and females, and then each one of the two groups has to be categorized as students, working graduates, unemployed graduates, and retired. These categories would allow for a reasonable analysis of the votes.

✓ Second we have to think of the hairstyle, and that will be by examining the ability to vote! In our new system, universities prepare legislation and explain and promote it through the media. Twenty days before the time of the referendum/election, the candidates have to present the reasons that make them better than each other, and the universities have to show the dangers of the legislation suggested by other universities. Five days before the elections, the evaluation of the voters' ability to vote will be performed by a test of questions that show that the voter has studied the subject or chosen the "don't care" option.

✓ Third we have to style our hair, and that will be by voting; now we can rest.

In our new system, an election/referendum must be performed every six months.

- The judicial authorities organize the public elections and the military elections.
- The military authorities organize the judicial elections.
- Voting is a must, and in every referendum there is "I don't agree on the system" entry.

Now, dear reader, do not hesitate to reread this chapter since I have done that five times to understand it even though I am the one who wrote it.

# ELEVENTH TRANSFORMATION

**Taxes**

In our new state, taxes cannot be imposed as in a dictatorship, not even as in current democratic systems. (No representation, no taxation.)

But it is based on the idea of **taxation after realization**.

No tax can be imposed except by the suggestion of the presidents of universities and decided by the half-yearly referendum. While local taxes have to be decided by the local half-yearly referendum, these local taxes may differ from one city to another.

The central taxes are divided into three groups:

1. The general tax, which can be classified according to different executive authority categories
2. The judicial tax
3. The military tax

All taxes are paid according to a percentage of one's personal wealth. Through the separation of taxes, we can ensure true independence of the authorities, and with the percentage of personal wealth, we will ensure justice—for the first time ever in history!

# Intimate Minds

## the fourth episode

*… Continued from page 31*

The year was 2039—sweet sixteen. At the age of sixteen, Sally was getting more and more attractive. Everybody wanted to get close to her and be her friend, but she did not feel close to anyone.

When she asked her dad why, he said, "Why don't you get more involved in social activities to be able to meet interesting people?"

It was then when she met the quarterback of a famous football team whom she liked. When he won a major game, he wanted to have sex with her. She almost responded to his request because he was a good partner in everything they did together.

She, however, was asking herself, "Why does he want to use my body during that moment that means a lot to him but not to me?" Sally then asked her friend, "Why didn't you ask for sex before?"

He replied, "You cannot imagine the pleasure I get from beating the other team."

Sally said, "Then have sex with the quarterback you have beaten." Deep down she knew that she was going to be a happy person one day.

It was time for the American soldier to return home, so he suggested that Mohammad volunteer in the American army so he would be able to return with him to the rich country. Their friendship would continue, and Mohammad would be able to get American citizenship because he served in the army. And so Mohammad joined the army and went to the rich country with the soldier. There he tried to participate with his friend in various activities, but the soldier restricted their friendship to sexual activities. Now Mohammad realized that their friendship was fake and that it only served the personal interests of the soldier, unlike what he recalled about friendship in his poor hometown. Friends, as he recalled, participate in almost all kinds of activities.

Mohammad told himself or was it that strange intuition, "I should have real friends so I can survive in this country." Mohammad later managed to build real friendships with his colleagues in the military.

*To be continued on page 47…*

# TWELFTH TRANSFORMATION

## Unification of the Armed Forces

Currently, the missions of the armed forces have become interlocked and complicated, with the army, the intelligence services, Special Forces, general security, police, customs, drug enforcement, and a force to fight terrorism, as well as an endless chain of additional organizations and expenses. What we know is that in all states and throughout history these military forces have failed; no government has been able to get rid of all dangers.

The reasons for this failure can be one of two or both:

1.  Innocent failure caused by a balance force between armed forces and the armed criminals
2.  Intentional failure to justify the continuation of the need for armed forces

The little advantages of the armed forces have not justified the huge disadvantages, which are expenses and interference of the armed forces in the government through coups d'état and the mistreatment of the civilians and others.

Our new system has the first *elected* military force, and it is the exclusive armed force of the state, so we have found the solution: the independence of this force so no politician can promote its leaders or pay their salaries. This means the real separation of authorities.

Therefore, the military will not interfere in issues of civilians except by a clear request by the authorized civilian judge, who will allow the use of force. Furthermore, the armed forces will have no right to investigate, interrogate, or prosecute any civilian. It will only help the civilian judge.

The jobs of the police, customs, general security, and drug enforcement will be transformed in our new system into civilian jobs. None of these civilians will have the right to carry a weapon.

One of my friends told me that the biggest oxymoron is "military intelligence." The elected military will not die for the sake of a religious man or a large corporation but will have the right and the ability to create military intelligence, not an oxymoron.

# Thirteenth Transformation

## Health Care

When I feel sick, many feelings run around my thoughts. I feel the need to pray, the need to be with my family, the need for silence, and the need for sunlight and the moon and the stars in the night, the need for fresh air. I don't want to speak about the health care in the United States, but it is very important for the reader to know that in the third world people may die at the entrance of the hospital for lack of money, and some cancer patients pay one year's income for fake, useless medicine.

*It's time to go to work.*

In a serene place in the middle of nature is where medical centers should be located; they should be designed as prefabricated rooms to one international standard, which would make them less expensive. And these rooms should have a special private external shape with a logo. The same logo and private shape should be given to the medical cars, boats, and airplanes, which would be manufactured especially for that purpose. In the middle of the same medical center is where medicine would be fabricated upon request. In the medical facility, any doctor or nurse could find things and know how everything worked without a special effort. In these medical centers, only doctors, nurses, pharmacists, and nutritionists are allowed to work. Therefore, they have to perform the jobs of management, maintenance, cleaning, and each and every other needed mission for medical services. The menial aspects of the medical center become part of the respected jobs (refer to the Nineteenth Transformation).

In our new state, all medical manufacturing is subject to international standards to ensure justice and low cost.

The private sector runs the centers while the government sets the prices. All medical services should be completely delivered upon request by any citizen, while paying bills should be done directly through banks; however, if the bank states that the citizen is not able to pay, at that point the government has to pay the bill. The government has to monitor the real medical services provided and their costs, as well as the real situation of a citizen who is not able to pay his bills. The money the government pays for medical coverage can be collected by special quarterly taxes, and the citizen who uses this coverage will be prohibited from the right to use or buy anything, which is referred to as a *luxury* until the citizen has repaid the government the money. The money will then be returned to the taxpayers in the following quarter.

And since the goal is to reduce the number of customers and the value of bills, there is no way for this system to succeed without having the government guarantee the profit of the privately owned medical centers through taxation.

Every human being should realize that the health issue should not be part of free trade and marketing, but it should be addressed from this perspective:

- Stopping demographic warfare and population growth
- Teaching and orienting societies and families to methods of proper nutrition
- Implementing the idea of preventive medical practices
- Teaching methods of personal, home, and general hygiene in the mandatory free-of-charge programs of education

# FOURTEENTH TRANSFORMATION

**Sports**

Sports had its beginnings as entertainment for kings. After centuries it became a way to earn a living by talented individuals and to make great profits by corporations. Sports also became a way for rulers and governments to distract the people from their reality. (Keep them fed and entertained: bread and circuses.) Today some kinds of sports have benefits to the body and the spirit, while excessive practice may result in some body damage caused by repetitive motion and some spiritual damage caused by using sports as a refuge to protect us from our social responsibilities. However, the danger of sports is in the permanent body disabilities that result from such sports as boxing or football, especially American football. What is more dangerous is in the spiritual damage caused by these sports. I still remember watching an American football game in which the knee of one of the players flipped upward as shown in the picture, and one of my friends' remark was, "The pleasure of inflicting pain." Don't we consider this spiritual destruction?

I think it is the right time to get rid of such games and encourage the new generations to practice civilized games like baseball, tennis, and others. If we don't want to stop playing American football, we must modify the rules to avoid direct personal contact.

I prefer to avoid professionalism and keep sports as a method to raise the spirit, maintain the body, and strengthen the relationship between people.

PS: This book is mine, and I can write whatever I want in it.

# Intimate Minds

**the fifth episode**

*… Continued from page 39*

It was the year 2041—hectic eighteen.

Sally met a guy who was an executive at her father's company. On a date with him at the beach, Sally was drinking a wine cooler when a cop passed by.

The cop said, "I have to arrest the owner of this bottle."

Sally replied, "Drinking alcohol is allowed in this area!"

The cop said, "But not in a glass container."

Sally said, "I did not know that."

The cop said, "Ignorance of the law is not an excuse. To whom does it belong?"

Sally admitted, "It's mine."

Even though her date knew that Sally had an exam the next day, he said, "Don't worry, Sally. I will tell your father and I'm sure he'll be able to postpone the date of your exam."

Sally heard that strange voice: "It was more appropriate for her date to say that the bottle was his own." Turning to her date Sally said, "No thanks. Since I'm under arrest, I will have enough time to call my dad."

Mohammad went to a private college. He was a bright and successful student and was able to compete with the top students. During the third semester, one of the professors was going very fast in his explanation, so fast that a significant number of students were unable to catch up. Even though Mohammad himself was not affected by the speed, he, with a number of the affected students, asked the administration to make the professor slow down a bit. The dean said the students should be more efficient in grasping the information.

Under the influence of that strange intuition Mohammad asked the dean, "Why, then, weren't the students subjected to a speed test during their entrance exam?"

That incident made Mohammad a popular guy among both students and professors.

*To be continued on page 56…*

# Fifteenth Transformation

**Law**

When I was twenty-five years old, a businessman I met in Liberia told me that the law was made by the bad guys to protect themselves. He told me this after someone stole $1 million from a group of companies that needed to transfer money out of Liberia. At that time, I was not convinced by what he said, and I was twenty-five years old. I am now fifty years, old and this is the second time I have mentioned my age in this book. I might mention it another time. My experience has showed me that the bad guys know how to benefit from law more than the good guys.

*Ignorance of the law is not an excuse.*

This expression is used all over the world, and I did not understand until now! It means that law protects those who know! Do those who know need the protection of law? The level of complications and the number of issues addressed by law leave us with a feeling that we are facing a maze that has no reason to exist. Do we need a law to prohibit us from having sex with dead people? And in some countries there are laws that allow males to have sex with female animals and prohibit them from having sexual relations with male animals. I am not an expert in law, and this book is not a place for such research. I propose simplifying laws so we don't let them interfere in each detail of our lives. Ethics, conscience, realization, culture, the tendency to get the best, parental feelings, and many other issues do not need laws to develop the human conscience. The need for law came along with the need for large societies, and law does not demolish conscience but does not stand without it.

The law should be easy and clear and deal with major issues. It should have harmony with conscience, which is what takes care of the little details.

Here is a practical idea. We should divide the law into two kinds:

- General law
- Private law

Examples of general law:

- Traffic law
- Laws that prohibit stealing, rape, kidnapping, etc.
- The state security
- Election law

These laws are tied to personal responsibility, where ignorance of the law is not an excuse. (General law is a mandatory subject in high school in the D.S.E.)

Examples of private law:

- Building law
- Commerce law
- Building maintenance
- Machine maintenance
- Health care law

These laws are tied to the company's responsibility, where ignorance of the law is not an excuse for companies. (Private law is taught in universities.)

In our new state, law does not allow for having insurance companies because these companies are corrupt and cause the disappearance of justice. In our new state, I can buy a car only from the manufacturing company, and I cannot sell it except to the manufacturing company while the company is always responsible for the maintenance of the car. But in the case of an accident, the responsibility will be on the manufacturing company if the reason has to do with the maintenance, and it will be on the driver if the reason has to do with negligence or bad driving performance.

In our new state, if the punishment is time in jail, it cannot be replaced by paying money or the other way around. The amount of money is always, just like taxes, a percentage of the personal wealth. No judge has the right to free a prisoner for payment of money, and in our new state, the right of fast prosecution is guaranteed, and here I am dreaming! In our new state, some of the laws are globalized for the sake of justice and equality (refer to page number 9 – Second Transformation). Here I am getting into a deep level of dreaming!

# Sixteenth Transformation

**Immigration**

Immigration is ancient. People have moved since the beginning of humankind. Today, since the establishment of nations, borders, and passports, we have no other choice than to put it under the microscope.

There is no doubt that immigration has presented an ideal solution to problems of some individuals of poor states and dictatorships. It has both some positive effects over the wealthy receiving countries and some negative results. For the receiving countries, the blend-in is very expensive and does not succeed in most cases. These are simple problems when compared to the kind of problems immigration causes poor countries: losing the best of their citizens and the hope of solving their problems. The poor and uneducated immigrants caused a big pain to the rich countries, but if we think of the number of immigrants who lost their lives crossing the river to the United States or crossing the Mediterranean Sea to Europe, we will discover a stunning catastrophe.

For better or worse, we say that the American dream is the dream of each and every realizing person in this world, and we have to admit that Americans have the right to worry about their standard of living and protect it.

And now let us start dreaming again. In our new state, immigration is subject to exchange[3] that will be of three kinds: experimental, temporary, or permanent. It will provide enrichment of the human experience. Since in our new system there will be no poor or wealthy

---

[3] Exchange immigration is to force an immigrant to find a citizen in the country he or she wants to immigrate to as a replacement.

state and no low-level jobs versus highly respected jobs, the need for immigration becomes an issue of wanting experience and getting to know the others through daily interactions. That is what ordinary tourism does not provide.

In our new state, there is no economic or political reason for immigration.

As for internal immigration, the danger lies in the immigration from the countryside to the cities and establishing random suburbs near wealthy cities. The phenomenon of random suburbs[4] is common to both wealthy and poor states.

In our new state, there are no big cities, and there are no neglected rural areas. Cities are not allowed to exceed one hundred thousand residents, and rural areas fall under the same political and economic regulations as the cities. Because of this new system, there will be no motivation for destructive immigration because the system of the new five cities (see the Fifth Transformation) provides a chance for every individual to choose what community answers his or her needs without teasing anybody else.

Good-bye to the old immigration, and I have to say to you that human suffering from immigration is much larger than all that wars and sickness have caused. Since I am a person who has experienced all of these difficulties, I don't think that a writer can deliver the picture because these sufferings have entered the fourth and the fifth dimensions. I need you to believe me.

---

[4] Random suburbs are crowded, poor neighborhoods built without any city planning, which become a stronghold for criminals.

# SEVENTEENTH TRANSFORMATION

## Every Big, Complicated Problem Has a Complicated Solution and an Easy Solution. Which Do You Choose?

We are going to talk about some complicated problems: terrorism, recycling, power conservation, conservation of raw materials, tax collection … Here is a solution: Every factory would be required to use an ID and a serial number on each and every product. This ID is made of a code of the country, a code of the manufacturing area, a code of the producing company, a code of the product, and the serial number, which should be issued by the government. The date of production and the validation period and the weight and size of the product should be issued by the company. And the product will remain the responsibility of the consumer unless the consumer returns it to the producer for recycling or rehabilitation or if the consumer doesn't need the product anymore.

And here, dear reader, you are asked to use your imagination and your ability to analyze or to get help from a friend so you can understand that a simple issue like ID can solve such complicated issues as the five problems we have mentioned.

You are right! This could not be a solution to these problems because the tax system is very complicated. Terrorists can smuggle explosive materials from countries of cheap flags,[5] while these countries do not know that they own this raw material and do not care about conserving energy or recycling.

---

[5] Cheap flags are countries that don't have any measures to ensure that the ships that are registered under their flag are not carrying smuggled goods or people.

If the concept of the new Democratic State of Environment spread all over this world, there would be no more cheap flag countries. Please, dear reader, do not forget that you are reading a book about science fiction.

The phenomenon of the cheap flag countries looks like the phenomena of random suburbs in some of the big cities. The same way I live my life, there would be no need for random suburbs. I was able to organize my furniture to get rid of the need for a maid, saved money, maintained my privacy with my family, and taught my kids by example that all the people should be maids for happiness and leisure (refer to page number 65 – Respectful Jobs). Happiness and leisure and all the desires of human spirit cannot come to reality except through sharing them with all we can see, hear, or reach.

In international relations, we should get rid of cheap flag countries because they are one of the causes of corruption and the disappearance of justice.

# Intimate Minds

## the sixth episode

*… Continued from page 47*

It was the year 2044—age twenty-one.

Sally's father introduced her to the chief operations officer, asking him to acquaint her with the business operations and help her to build leadership.

During the tour throughout the various departments of the company, Sally asked the COO, "Who or what determines the number of departments in the company?"

He said, "This is the toughest issue in leadership because this structure should allow all the departments to accomplish their tasks without having to understand the whole job's concept."

Sally said, "How would the job be efficient without understanding the whole job's concept?"

The COO said. "You are right, but this inefficiency would be at the expense of the employees only and not the company. This issue is the toughest in leadership. Your father told me once that business is the art of manipulating people." Is it telepathy? Sally heard the voice telling her that this isn't leadership, but what would it be then?

It was graduation day, and Mohammad was so excited, looking forward to that moment. Yet he was sad and heartbroken because he was unable to locate his father. During the last year, he got in touch with some Afghani students in an attempt to locate his father. While he was entering the graduation ceremony, he was arrested by an anti-terrorist force. Earlier, Mohammad had bought a small amount of a chemical substance he needed for his senior project. Unfortunately that same chemical was used by an Afghani terrorist group to make a bomb. The terrorists' intention was to avenge those who were killed by the American army. Among those Afghanis Mohammad had contacted was a member of that terrorist group.

During the interrogation, the officer said, "You bought the chemical that was used by the terrorists, and we have a video as evidence."

Mohammad said, "That is true. I used it in my senior project."

The officer said, "Have you used it up?"

Mohammad replied, "No."

The officer said, "Then where is the rest of the material?"

Mohammad said, "It's in the collage lab." Mohammad didn't know how these words came to his mouth. It was probably that strange voice again that came to his rescue.

*To be continued on page 72…*

# Eighteenth Transformation

I remember the days when I was a student at DeVry University twenty years ago. I was asked to write a paper about leadership. At that time I wrote that leadership had been practiced throughout history as "the art of promoting fear," and that this art was practiced by the profiteers and the leaders. I cannot forget President Bush's speech after the end of the Cold War when he said, "Our new enemy is uncertainty." I felt at that time that victory is worthless if it means replacing the enemy with another enemy. Also in that paper I concluded that leadership should be by example, but today I have a different view, which follows.

Every action motivated by fear is an unbalanced reaction. I will begin with what the leader is not. The leader should not direct our vision to a fearful issue, nor should the leader think for us or teach us how to think; the leader should not be the one who provides a good example. This world is full of leaders who failed to prevent September 11 and failed to bring Osama Bin Laden to an open court procedure. I have not been able to understand the real reason for the historical struggle between Arabs and Jews. None of the citizens of the democratic states were able to understand the reason for the existence of the giant state of China and the midget state of Singapore. None of them understood why they had to save money to go to Bali,[6] where they would be entertained by terrorists and lose their lives. Today I'm fifty years old and I am always trying to see that the great scientific accomplishments will raise the level of human lives.

We have developed the cellular phone many times, but we did not try to develop the democratic system in a way to allow American citizens

---

[6] Bali is a resort that was attacked by terrorists.

to understand, for example, that when they elect a president (without realizing the level of influence the United States has over the dictator regimes in the world), they decide the continuity of dictator regimes from which some big companies benefit.

The world is full of knowledge, but it's not accessible to those who are trying to raise the level of human lives. Knowledge is a result of research. Research needs money, money is with big corporations, and big corporations create or cut down jobs just to increase their fortune. The D.S.E. universities would do research to raise the level of human lives with the least possible working hours.

The leader should be the one who can convince a group of people to use knowledge to improve their lives.

## DEFINITION

We can choose one of the following definitions:

1. Leadership is the art of implementing knowledge.
2. Leadership is the art of implementing knowledge in a specific subject and for a specified period of time.

Any person, no matter how successful he/she is, will be affected by a particular incident until he or she dies. For that reason, leadership should be temporary. We have to free history from the individual's prison. We should not think of leadership as it is now because it is disabling our brains, but we should think about it as specified and temporary, *and it resides in each and every one of us.*

The role of schools and universities is very important in developing leaders. In our new state, schools and universities that belong to the private sector will be mandated to teach basic education, which covers the ability to read and write one language, basic arithmetic, general law, hygiene, rights, duties, and leadership. These subjects are to be free of charge. After that, it is up to the parents to add more subjects, which they have to pay for.

This is a place for science fiction to work!

# Nineteenth Transformation

When we talk about ethics, we may find some distinctions in the concepts and the ways to understand them. Sometimes we may even find conflicts since some people consider ethics to be an existential issue and others consider it a religious issue, while many people just inherited it as an influence of history. Here we are not looking for scientific research to give a definition of ethics; all we are going to do is to sort out some issues using an existential perspective so we can reach what can be considered a friendly environment for ethics to grow.

When we talked about law, we said that it can never come to effect without ethics (refer to page number 49 – Law). Here, we will explain how law can be *in the service of ethics without sentence or punishment.*

## The Twelve Commandments

### Memories of Neighborhood

Settlement was the foundation of civilization until civilization turned to push us again toward immigration, looking for job opportunities or security or medical care or just the need to do things in the presence of people who we don't know and who don't know us. Memories of one's neighborhood are what results from belonging to a family, having relatives and friends. The effect this little group of humans may have on a place and the effect of the place on this little group result in a common mood and a distinct personality. This feeling of belonging to a group and the intimate knowing of a place can be the state of safety that we are naming "the memory of the neighborhood." So *destruction of a neighborhood should be outlawed,* and if it has to be developed, the development should not affect the neighborhood's personality.

## AVOIDING CROWDS

A person who did not try to live in a two-room house for a family of ten, or the one who did not stay in a prison cell that is made to house five prisoners and have to share it with thirty, or the one who did not ride a train with a hundred seats with one thousand passengers may not understand the effect of *crowdedness* on the human spirit.

Outlawing *crowdedness* helps the individual feel his or her value and feel the respect given by the society so the respect can be mutual. And to achieve this state of sufficient room, we should start by reducing the rate of population growth on a global level and dismantle the large cities and then outlaw the multifamily buildings. We are considering having to get an electronic reservation before using the highway. Give me my space.

## Permanent Ownership of a House

This commandment guarantees the right of every individual to own a lot, on which one can *build a house surrounded by a garden.* This lot is not subject to any taxation, and neither the state nor the judicial system, nor even the military authorities, have the right to take ownership away from the individual for any reason whatsoever. Because of the fair distribution of property, we will have no more homeless people, and thus we rid ourselves of diseases a homeless person can carry and spread. We rid ourselves of worrying about becoming homeless. What is more important is that tenants will be relieved of the worries of paying rent, buyers from the worries of paying mortgages, owners from the worries of taxes, and *heirs* from the worries of sharing the inheritance.

## House Farming

What is the relation between patience and ethics?

House farming is work that could be shared among family members and creates a good reason for interaction between neighbors and friends while it does not need full occupation since a person can perform some of it in the early morning and this could be considered as a morning workout or after work. One of the most important benefits of house farming is getting rid of organic waste. Also, house farming gives humans a better chance for nutritional diversity by growing much of one's own food. Further, it reduces pollution and guarantees the increase of green areas between houses. Finally, the most important thing is that *house farming teaches patience.* We need patience so that we don't answer our husbands or wives when we are angry, so divorce will not happen. We need patience so we can build a fortune by hard work, so we will not steal. Are you patient enough to understand the relationship between patience and ethics?

## PROPER DIET

If we consider that ethics is an issue that has to do with the interactions between individuals, so let us imagine this interaction that will not have any positive results except for the ability of individuals to exchange benefits. *What benefits could we expect from a hungry person?* The relationship between the kind of food we eat and the abilities to analyze, endure, and control our attitude, sexual, and athletic performance is no secret. There is equal importance between getting the nutrients we need and the method by which we get the nutrients. Everyone knows that the pleasure that comes from eating tasty food is equivalent and as necessary as sharing it with someone we love, as well as the way food is presented and offered. Do we have to ask ourselves if we enjoy using our bare hands to eat more than using a fork made of metal, or had we better ask ourselves if it is acceptable to still have starvation in this world?

## Economic Competition

Competition is a natural motivator for production and work, but it can become dangerous when competition turns into fighting. The difference is that competition occurs between someone successful and someone who is more successful. The ethical problem occurs at the expense of someone else, even at their destruction. People who have worked in a company anywhere in the world know that *almost 80 percent of their effort goes to what is known as office politics.*

Laws in companies and laws of labor should get rid of destructive competition.

## Respectful Jobs

Any quick observation of how jobs and missions are divided in both wealthy and poor countries clearly uncovers the existence of important jobs and low-level jobs. Any quick analysis of how these low-level jobs are performed can show how they cause a loss of energy and a big burden to the economy and the environment, which is avoidable.

I watched the way domestic help work in many countries, with the excessive use of cleaning material and in some of the cases dangerous mixing of these materials, where the level of hygiene was not acceptable. The reason was often not the inability of the worker but the indifference. Having domestic help is an invasion of the house's privacy, and it develops a feeling of superiority in the mind of the employer (especially in third-world countries).

If we dismantle this job, we can turn it into a group of specialties performed by different companies in a respectful manner, which guarantees that no instruction will be given directly from the owner of the house to the workers so a company takes care of the carpets and curtains, another company cleans doors and windows, and a different company takes care of restrooms and other things. The important thing is that all jobs should be redesigned to become respectful, and only at that time we can say that the age of slavery is over.

## PERSONAL TIME/TIMES

In the third world time has no value whatsoever, while in the Western world a high value is placed on time. I don't know how to be a philosopher, so I can announce a new understanding of time, but I am a good time waster, and I still remember many moments of my life when I wished that time could end. Now let us come back to ethics. Personal time is an essential need for growth and the development of ethics most probably. Our economic systems should *allow us to give our kids what they may need of our time,* so we can monitor their growth and they can view our lives. We should give the lover, the friend, the neighbor, the colleague, and the relative the time they need. What is more important is that the economic systems should allow us to listen to music and to exercise and to farm and go to museums and theaters and beaches and watch nature till we learn how to purify our conduct.

## Music and What Follows

Music and all that follows in art from singing, dancing, painting, sculpture, films, plays, and designing cars (even washing dishes since art exists in everything), has its special ability to purify the spirit and make it ethical. There are many kinds of music that have a positive influence, and there are other kinds that have the opposite influence. Hasn't it occurred to anybody that we could benefit from modern science to test the effect of music and classify it in the same way movies are rated?

## Sports

We have mentioned before that some sports can be harmful and some sports can be beneficial (refer to page number 45 – Sports). Here we

need to refer to an important issue: if we consider that strengthening family relations, friendships, work relationships, and patriotism is based on mutual benefits, so we see that physical abilities have a major role in life. *Physical activity is a reason for and a result of the love of living.*

## GROUP WORK DURING CATASTROPHES

The strongest friendships occur between individuals during chaos resulting from kidnapping or a collapsed building or a natural disaster. Why should we wait for disasters? We can do better! Organizing an activity of simulating a disaster can make a person feel the importance of group work and the importance of belonging to a neighborhood. Regarding the meaning of this simulation, assuming it is an earthquake, for example, we would perform rescue missions: moving, gathering, counting, locating the needed tools for rescue. There are people who have specialized in hazardous conditions and can be consulted to explain the details. What is important here is that we should promote all kinds of volunteer group work to strengthen the community spirit.

## SEXUAL STABILITY

This is the most complicated commandment. Only blinding lights are used to uncover the dark tunnels of the sexual issues and the result. The issue of sex has been the subject of much interference throughout written history. It started from the need of tribes to protect their offspring, and then the appearance of prostitution passing by the religious constraints became state laws, and the result most probably was not acceptable! We said it is a complicated issue because it is governed by mystery, and we cannot unveil this mystery; most probably we should not. This is what I think! But if we gathered all we know about incidents of rape and cheating in relations and prostitution and the exchange of diseases and sexual harassment, there is enough to be sure that we do have a problem.

When I was studying at the university, I had a discussion about interracial marriages. Among the participants was a psychology professor (a female professor who had raised a male child), yet she didn't know that the male may be subject to a painful development in the nipples as a result of puberty around the age of twelve. The professor said that the cultural contradiction between races may be a reason for the failure of interracial marriages. Then I told her that the distance in culture between men and women in the same race is much larger than the distance in culture between races. Men and women should get to know each other much more than they do now, and I think this will contribute to reduced sexual problems.

Maybe the sense of domination has many negative effects on sexual relations. This sense of domination is what our primitive brains offered as the relationship with the struggle for survival. The new Democratic State of Environment may help in reducing the effect of "the struggle for survival" by pushing it away from its individual primitive nature to a socially improved nature, and this will take away the need for dominance.

I think that I do have the courage to enter the tunnels of the sexual problem, but I don't have all the experience. Here the expertise of psychologists, sociologists, religious leaders, and legislators is needed to develop means to achieve sexual stability.

I don't claim to have the solution for the problem, but sexual stability is the elimination of rape, cheating in relations, prostitution, sexual harassment, etc.

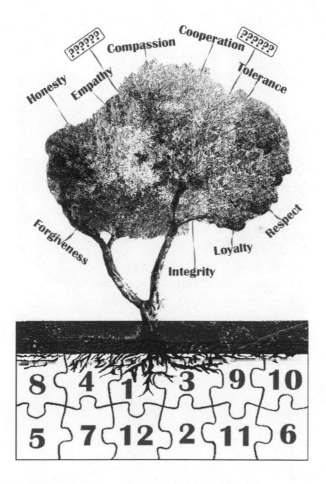

Nobody can manufacture ethics and moral values, which are living elements that need a friendly environment to nourish and grow. These twelve commandments are what I think compose that friendly environment. Some of these commandments need legislation, but some need more research and development.

# Intimate Minds

**the seventh episode**

*… Continued from page 56*

The year 2048—age twenty-five.

Sally's father asked, "Why aren't you happy?"

Sally replied, "I believe it's because I'm rich."

Astonished by her answer, her father said, "Because you're rich! I don't get you."

Sally explained, "When I refused to work at your company, it was because I wanted to be treated as any other person. It didn't take me long, however, to realize that nothing goes on naturally there or elsewhere."

Her father said, "Still I can't understand."

Sally said, "Why, for example, do we need an employee to make coffee for us although we can find pleasure in doing this job by ourselves?"

Her father said, "Are you trying to tell me that you are happy only when you make your own coffee by yourself?"

Sally said, "What does fortune mean to you, Dad? Can you tell me?"

Her father said, "Well, I haven't really thought about that, but I believe it's the result of my passion for success, which I had ever since I was a child."

Sally asked, "But what have I done to deserve this fortune? Why does everyone seek it? And what about you, Dad? Was it fortune that made you happy? Or was it success?"

Her father replied, "I think happiness comes from success."

The voice was again whispering to Sally's ear, "You would be happy if you managed to abolish all disrespected jobs in the world."

Mohammad worked at a recycling company. His ambition was to understand all the details about the company so that one day he could have a recycling company of his own. While working, he noticed that the dismantling of a certain product required some information from the manufacturing company so the recycling process would be done appropriately.

When Mohammad discussed this issue with the owner of the company, he said, "Don't worry! This recycled by-product goes to the cheap flag countries (third world)."

Mohammad smiled and said, "My own father is a citizen of a cheap flag country."

The company owner then said, "I apologize. I meant no offense."

Mohammad said, "All that I remember about Afghanistan is my loving and caring father and that I got lost in the big city, and the American soldier who helped me and gave me the chance to come to America."

The owner of the company then said, "Do you consider yourself an American, or do you still have loyalty to Afghanistan?"

Mohammad answered, "My loyalty is to America because this is the place where I felt accepted and appreciated."

The owner of the company asked, "What about your father?"

Mohammad said, "When I get the needed money, I will go to Afghanistan and look for him."

The company owner said, "America did a great job in helping Afghanistan."

At this moment telepathy from Sally gave Mohammad this thought: *I'm not sure if Afghanistan needed our help at that time, but I'm sure that it does need help now, and there's nothing we can do about it.*

*To be continued on page 77…*

# CONCLUSION

When we succeed in replacing the residents of the planet, there will be no more humans. It will be filled with angels, for the Democratic State of Environment will have become a reality.

In our new state, the distinguished individuals will remain as a positive and realistic issue, and the individuals will learn that happiness is in using moments. The new concept of state allows all those who have ambition to build different kinds of states to build their states without having to cause bloodshed or torturing, and *if the there is a disagreement about the use of the expression "the state," we can agree on a different expression.*

Dear reader, I want you to accept me as a leader during your reading of this book because I want to show you the method to obey nature and the highest level of personal wealth and the elected military and the little government, which leaves productivity to individuals and the private sector and globalizing personal ownership laws and the laws of election, and since I am not a professional writer, I want you to reread this book if you find in it what is good and accept me as a leader during reading. When you are done reading, you can even forget my name.

# Intimate Minds

## the final episode

... *Continued from page 72*

It was the year 2051—age twenty-eight.

Mohammad became the owner of a recycling company. He became famous after designing a car that takes its color from its computer through fiber optics and that can be simply cleaned by sand paper instead of water. As for Sally, who returned to work with her father, she managed to make an agreement with him to build a university whose mission is to design respected jobs in companies. Only then did she start to feel happy.

Once during the graduation of the students, she met Mohammad, who was invited because his company made a large financial contribution to the university.

Sally said, "I feel that I've known you since a long time ago."

Mohammad responded, "That's exactly what I feel too."

Sally said, "I don't remember your face or your voice, but I would like to know you better."

Mohammad said, "Do you know what makes your face so different?"

"Tell me," said Sally.

Mohammad said, "Your face reminds me of the American actress Rachel as she looked in a picture I saw in a Beverly Hills Store."

Sally said, "Really? No one ever said that to me before."

Mohammad added, "Actually there's a sort of alliance between dream and intelligence in her face and in yours as well. It is so strong that one cannot tell if you are dreaming or creating."

Rachel

*The End!*

Mr. Ramzi Saab's manuscript proposes an unorthodox approach to solve the penuries of the different societies and the world at large, which, until this moment, have been suffering from suffocating economic policies where the only thing achieved was the destruction of the environment and the transformation of humans into mere slaves to the wage. Mr. Saab's proposal is based on a more humane and environmentally friendly approach, where the latter is the base and focus of his novel idea. He named this system *the Democratic State of Environment*.

This system, which has the environment as its core, includes different facets where the most important one is the economic facet. Economics in this system requires a complete amalgamation of the governments and the private sectors. This would be achieved by mixing the command economy and the free market economy. Here governments/ states have no right to perform any kind of productivity, narrowing its role to draw the main guidelines delineating ceilings and floors within which the private sector (industrialists, agriculturalists, businesses, etc.) will have the complete freedom to compete with each other and generate their respective regulated profits.

To achieve what was mentioned in the previous lines, the core and focus of this socioeconomic spectrum is technological advancement, which will help in the reduction of goods production, stock handling, and waste by-products since anything desired can be computer generated and virtually tried before spending a penny on its actual physical manufacture. Along this technological base, currency will no longer be supported/backed by mineral resources (gold, oil, etc.)

but on an empiric/intrinsic energy value that will be decided by the council of university.

Dr. Elie Michel Maalouf,
General Director
Government Commissioner to the Lebanese Central Bank

The text is boiling with surprising, brave, brainstorming, and rather nightmarish ideas that may belong to the future but definitely not to the present. As a lawyer and friend of nature, I do appreciate your novel and munificent suggested bond between democracy and environment. However, science fictional concepts are hard for me to digest for the time being.

Issam Naaman,<br>
Lawyer, writer, and former minister of telecommunications,<br>
Lebanon, 2016